Introduction

The word apartheid means "separateness" and since 1948 when the concept of apartheid was officially written into the statute book, a total separation of the races has been enforced by South Africa's white rulers. A white minority of less than five million controls a total population of 36 million whites, Africans, coloureds, Indians and others. The white 13 per cent of the population owns 87 per cent of the land. The apartheid laws have restricted where the black majority can live. Most whites enjoy a very high standard of living, while most blacks live in dire poverty.

Against this background of inequality it is hardly surprising that blacks of South Africa have organised resistance to the all-dominant whites. After their initial military defeat by the European settlers by the beginning of this century, the black people first tried diplomacy. As the Nationalist government became increasingly determined to resist their peaceful opposition, the people eventually took up arms. The Sharpeville massacre of unarmed demonstrators in 1960 was a turning point. Since then there have been a succession of uprisings, starting with the Soweto revolt of 1976. Appalled by the determination of the whites to cling to apartheid whatever the cost, the international world finally took action and imposed effective sanctions on South Africa after 1984.

In 1990 President Frederik Willem de Klerk announced dramatic reforms aimed at preserving white power but making concessions to blacks in order to reduce internal and international opposition. The African National Congress (ANC), the Pan-Africanist Congress (PAC) and the South African Communist Party (SACP) were unbanned, paving the way for a series of talks between the government and the ANC. But Inkatha leader Gatsha Buthelezi felt threatened by the ANC's popularity, and conflict flared in the Transvaal when Inkatha supporters attacked township residents who largely supported the ANC. At least 700 people were killed in the late summer.

The international community had agreed to lift sanctions when change in South Africa was "irreversible", but there is disagreement about what this means. The changes introduced go some way to removing apartheid but fall short of introducing democratic majority rule. Meanwhile South Africa faces the prospect of escalating violence in the townships. Much blood is likely to be shed before apartheid is buried.

Foundations of apartheid

Apartheid began with European colonial expansion in Africa from 1652 onwards. Although the Dutch and British settlers fought each other later on, they were united in oppressing black people.

The Dutch settlement

Under apartheid, South African school children have been taught that the history of their country started in 1652, when the Dutchman Jan van Riebeeck landed at the Cape of Good Hope, at the southern tip of Africa. The Dutch were building up their wealth by trading and needed the Cape settlement to resupply their ships.

At the Cape lived the Khoikhoi (whom the Europeans called "Hottentots") and the San (or "Bushmen"). Further inland, and moving ever southwards in search of more grazing land for their cattle, were the Xhosa, Zulu and other Nguni tribes, and the Sotho and Tswana peoples. Shortly after their arrival, the Dutch settlers seized the lands and cattle of the original inhabitants of the Cape.

When the Khoikhoi and the San defended their lands and cattle with bows, arrows and spears, the white settlers set about systematically exterminating them. The Khoikhoi became almost extinct, and only a few San survived. The Dutch settlers, known as the Boers, were unable to subdue the Xhosa people living further inland so they imported slaves from Malaya and elsewhere to do manual work at the Cape. In 1805 the British seized the Cape in order to protect their spice trade and sea route to the Far East. In 1820 about 4,000 settlers from Britain landed on the coast about 800 km east of Cape Town.

△ In 1652 the Dutch sent an 80-strong company to build a fort on the Cape of Good Hope. The Dutch were there to supply Dutch fleets on their journey to the Far East. The colony thrived and spread further inland, taking over land for agriculture.

4

HOTSPOTS

SOUTH AFRICA
THE END OF APARTHEID?

JOAN BRICKHILL

A GLOUCESTER PRESS BOOK

Contents

In 1652 the Dutch set up a settlement on the southern tip of South Africa. The British arrived in force at the beginning of the 19th century and by 1910 white supremacy had been established in that region.

After 1910 successive governments took away black people's rights. In 1948 the National Party swept into power and brought in apartheid laws.

Black people responded to apartheid by trying to organise themselves non-violently. When the white government used violence against them they turned to armed struggle.

Since 1990 the leader of the National Party has started to repeal apartheid laws but will this really be the end of apartheid?

▷ In October 1989 South African trade unionists took part in a mass demonstration. Since the first state of emergency was declared in 1986, large demonstrations had been banned. The fact that the South African government allowed black people to protest against its power was a firm indication that apartheid in South Africa was undergoing change.

▽ These present-day Zulus are the descendants of the warrior peoples of South Africa. During the late 18th century a Zulu kingdom was set up by conquest. It survived until it was defeated by the British in the late 19th century.

European colonisation

The British Army succeeded where the Boers had failed: they defeated the Xhosa and other African tribes living along the east coast. By the end of the 19th century, the Europeans had seized nearly nine-tenths of what is now called South Africa. The result was that the Africans could no longer make a living by farming the remaining one-tenth independently. Black people were also often subject to pass laws, which controlled where they lived and who they worked for. Many of them were forced to work as farm labourers for the white settlers.

Britain's colonial expansion in the southern tip of Africa was not achieved without cost to British lives. At the Battle of Isandhlwana on 22 January 1879, the Zulus scored the greatest victory by warriors over a "modern" army. Armed with only spears and shields, the Zulu army killed 1,800 British soldiers.

It took a century after the British annexed the Cape to complete the conquest of the original inhabitants of South Africa. They fought many wars of resistance. The last one occurred in 1906 when the Zulus rose up in the Bambata rebellion. Those who lost their lands as a result of these wars have continued to fight against white rule for 350 years. Had the tribes not fought among themselves, this resistance might have been more successful.

British/Boer conflict

British rule of the Cape Colony antagonised the Boers. In the century and a half of Dutch settlement before the British arrived, many of the settlers had developed a very independent, isolated and semi-nomadic way of life as cattle herders. Many of them had received little education. Many Boers came to regard themselves as God's chosen people, and saw their military victories as confirmation from God that they were special. They believed hard manual work was the black people's lot; they justified this with an obscure quotation from the Bible, which said that blacks were descendants of the children of Ham, destined to be "hewers of wood and drawers of water".

It was no wonder then that the Boers should have resented coming under the authority of the British at the start of the 19th century. Britain had been undergoing 50 years of Industrial Revolution and was the world's leading industrial power with the largest and most efficient navy. The British brought with them new ideas, in tune with the changes occurring in Europe.

The Great Trek

One of these "new" ideas was that slavery was wrong. In December 1833 all slaves within the British empire were freed under a law passed in Britain. This was the last straw for the Boers. Some 6,000 left the colony between 1835 and 1840 in what became known as the Great Trek. Within 20 years, the Boers had established themselves far to the north of the Cape, founding their own republics (the main two were known as the Transvaal or South African Republic and the Orange Free State). Both states were based on the idea that there could be no equality between black and white. Thus began the long-running rivalry between Boer and British. During the second half of the 19th century the division became increasingly bitter after the discovery of great mineral wealth in South Africa.

Diamond fever

The discovery of diamonds in 1867-68 along the Orange and Vaal Rivers set off the greatest diamond rush in history. Three years later diamonds were found deep underground in Kimberley. Britain annexed the diamond-rich territory of the Griqua people in 1871. This was followed by the discovery in 1886 of vast gold deposits in the Transvaal area.

In South Africa the mineral deposits were so large and so deep that small independent diggers could not exploit them. Deep-level mining required a huge labour force and a substantial amount of money. Large companies soon controlled the diamond fields. Small companies formed bigger ones or went bankrupt, until the few that remained merged to form one huge corporation, De Beers Consolidated Mines. By the 1890s, De Beers controlled 90 per cent of the world's output of diamonds.

British businessman Cecil Rhodes, chairman of De Beers, and other mining magnates made considerable fortunes. Not only were the diamond and gold deposits extremely rich but the companies had a plentiful supply of labour for the exhausting and dangerous work underground. The miners were paid very low wages.

The diamond mining companies introduced the migrant labour system to South Africa. Local black peasant farmers did not want to work in the mines, so workers were recruited from neighbouring territories, particularly from Mozambique. The companies set up housing compounds where their black workers were forced to live in appalling conditions without their families.

The Boer War
During the war, the British burned down Boer farmsteads and confiscated cattle, to stop supplies reaching the guerrilla fighters. The destitute and homeless Boer families were put in the first "concentration camps", where 20-26,000 of them died. This left a deep legacy of bitterness against the British among the Boers, today's Afrikaners.

▽ Every year Afrikaner people celebrate the anniversary of the Great Trek by recreating the event. By 1840, 6,000 Afrikaner people had left the Cape Colony and settled further inland. They took their Khoikhoi servants and former slaves with them.

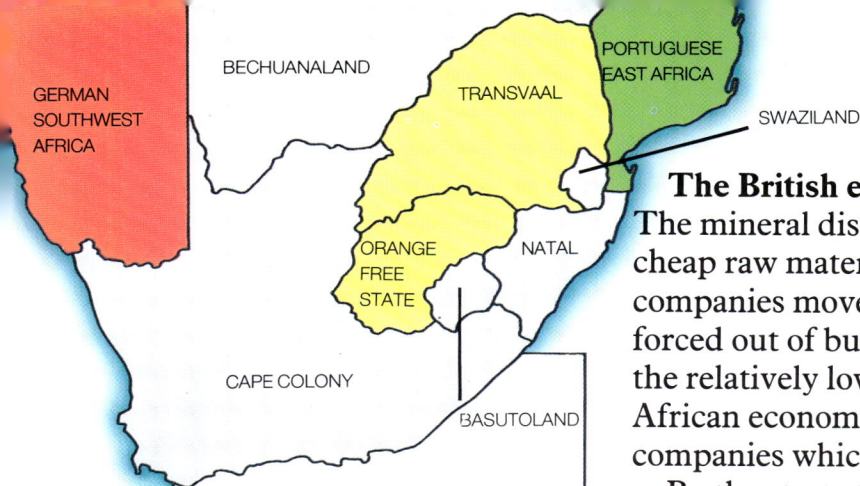

▨ (yellow)	Boer republics
▢ (white)	British colonies
▨ (green)	Portuguese colonies
▨ (red)	German colonies

△ The map shows the division of southern Africa in the 19th century into Boer republics and European colonies. The Boer republics lost their independence to the British during the Boer War.

The British expand northwards

The mineral discoveries gave Britain the chance to acquire cheap raw materials for its expanding industry. British companies moved in swiftly. Smaller companies were again forced out of business because of lack of finance for mining the relatively low grade, deep-level gold ore. The South African economy came to be dominated by a few large companies which formed the Chamber of Mines in 1887.

By the start of the 20th century, the white settlers had taken over most of South Africa's land and mineral wealth. The original inhabitants had been uprooted, their traditional means of subsistence had been destroyed, families had been torn apart by the migrant labour system and many worked in the factories, mines and homes of their conquerors.

The Boer War

While the British companies dominated the goldfields of the South African Republic (what is now the Transvaal province of South Africa), political control was exercised by the Boers in the independent Boer republics. The British wanted political power in the region. War broke out between the British and the Boers in 1899. The British annexed the other independent Boer republic, the Orange Free State, in May 1900 and occupied Johannesburg, the centre of the goldfields in the South African Republic. They annexed the republic itself on 1 September. The Boers then fought a guerrilla war against the powerful British army, inflicting severe losses – 4,000 Boer lives were lost compared with 5,774 British soldiers killed in action and 16,168 who died of wounds and disease.

The White Union

One British justification for waging this costly war of aggression had been to protect the interests of black people in the Boer republics. However, the peace terms made it clear that power would stay in the hands of the white minority. In 1910 the former Boer republics and British colonies of Natal and the Cape were joined together and given independence within the British empire as the Union of South Africa. The British government agreed that the question of whether blacks would be allowed to vote would be left for the whites in South Africa to decide. The British and the Afrikaners soon formed an alliance based on white supremacy; they found common ground in the dispossession and exploitation of black South Africans.

Setting up the apartheid state

The year 1948 saw the birth of the apartheid state.

Founding the African National Congress (ANC)

Black people realised that the white Union of South Africa would only look after white interests. In 1912 they responded by setting up a national organisation to campaign against white domination. The people who decided to form the African National Congress (then called the Native National Congress) were an educated group who did not want to overthrow white rule but wanted the whites to accept black people. They wanted a non-racial society.

The 1913 Land Act

A year after this black people suffered a major loss of rights when a new land act was passed. The 1913 Natives Land Act made it illegal for Africans to buy land outside the seven to eight per cent of territory (known as reserves) set aside for them. The white minority government set aside these reserves for Africans and this formed the basis for the "Bantustan" (or homelands) system of later years. The new law also stopped the practice of whites leasing land to black people outside the reserves. As a result many Africans were driven off their land and made homeless. Black farmers found it more difficult to make a living farming and many were driven to seek jobs working for white bosses. In the reserves people were increasingly unable to grow enough food for themselves and African farming was gradually destroyed. The 1913 and 1936 Land Acts eventually created a divided South Africa, where the white minority "legally" owned 87 per cent of the land.

△ After the 1913 Land Act many African farmworkers were left without the land that they had previously rented from white landowners. They were forced to leave their homes and live on reserves, or else work for white farmers for very low wages. If the farmworkers tried to leave for better paid jobs in town, the farmers would use their influence to prevent the farmworkers from getting a "pass", which would allow them to leave.

The 1913 Land Act
The act listed areas totalling 22 million acres, or about seven per cent of the area of South Africa, as reserves for black people. The act also called for a commission to look into land ownership. It proposed that 18 million more acres be set aside, but white people protested and nothing was done.

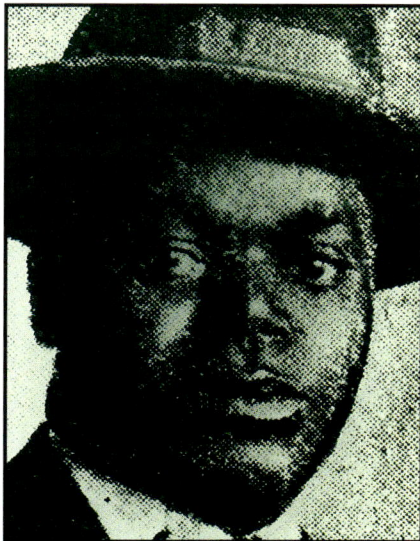

△ Pixley ka Isaka Seme was one of the founders of the Native National Congress (later known as the ANC). It was formed to campaign against the proposed introduction of the Land Act. In 1912 Seme said "We have called you therefore to this conference so that we can devise ways and means of forming our national union for the purpose of creating national unity and defending our rights and privileges."

Building up black opposition

In its early years the ANC leaders were unable to make much impact on white minority rule. They believed that they could win acceptance from the whites by persuasion and did not even demand the right to vote for all black people. The ANC retained its faith in Britain and continued to appeal in vain for protection by sending delegations and petitions to London. This confidence survived in spite of the fact that Britain had allowed the formation of a white-ruled South African state, and in 1936 had agreed that black Africans should be removed from the electoral roll in the Cape province. The ANC's polite appeals failed to change white policy; instead, repression and discrimination against blacks increased.

The 1914-18 war in Europe stimulated industrial growth in South Africa and many blacks went to the cities in search of work. The white government responded to these changes by passing a new law, the 1923 Natives (Urban Areas) Act. This laid down the principle that blacks living in towns could only live in segregated areas and the numbers of blacks in urban areas should be strictly controlled. In spite of this law black people became Africa's largest working class. For most of the first half of the century, black workers organised around trade unions and the Communist Party, which was formed in 1921 from the left-wing of the white labour movement. By 1928 the Communist Party had a mainly black membership and concentrated on building black trade unions.

The Pact government

Although there was much antagonism between Afrikaners and the English-speaking whites (backed by Britain) after the union, it did not prevent them from uniting in a common cause against their black compatriots. During the 1920s and 1930s government passed from one white party to the other and back again. A Pact (or coalition) government of the Afrikaner Nationalist Party and the small white Labour Party took power from the South African Party (SAP), which reflected some British and mining interests, in 1924. The Pact government concentrated on protecting white workers from black competition and the position of black people worsened.

English economic domination

Throughout the period English-speaking whites dominated the economy, while the Afrikaners, who made up 60 per cent of the whites, were the most important political force. Afrikaner nationalist politicians encouraged their community to invest in firms and buy from the shops of their own people. These moves were designed to ensure the Afrikaners "caught up" with the English, who had all the advantages of British capital, technology, skills and international connections.

It was only after the Afrikaner nationalists achieved political power in 1924 and used it to promote Afrikaners that the economic gap between them and the English-speaking whites began to narrow significantly.

△ In January 1922 white miners went on strike because they wanted to stop the mining companies from using lower paid Africans to do their work. Black workers were paid 15 times less than whites. The strike lasted until March when the South African government came down on the mine owners' side and sent in the army. In the ensuing fighting 153 were killed and 687 injured. Jan Smuts' South African Party became very unpopular after this and lost the 1924 election.

Afrikaner nationalism and black resistance

The Afrikaner Nationalist Party tried to win Afrikaner voters on the basis of their economic disadvantages, past injustices and what was called the "*swart gevaar*" (the black threat). The majority of Afrikaners eventually rallied behind the Afrikaner Nationalist Party, and government passed into their hands. But the English-speakers still owned most of the industrial and commercial wealth.

Economic problems resulting from the worldwide Great Depression of the 1930s eventually drove the Nationalists into coalition with the SAP in 1933. Soon the two merged to form the United Party. However, a core of Afrikaner nationalists, who sympathised with German Nazi beliefs of racial superiority, refused to join the United Party and formed their own National Party.

The Afrikaner Nationalists sweep to power

During the Second World War (1939-45) black workers were called on to take up jobs formerly held by whites because of a shortage of labour. This was accompanied by a massive growth in the number of African people living in towns. Both trends allowed the ANC to build up its strength. In 1942 a group of young African nationalists within the ANC, including Nelson Mandela and Oliver Tambo, became tired of the timidity of their leaders and formed an ANC Youth League to push for more militant action. Some of the controls on African workers were, in fact, relaxed during the war by the government. The wartime prime minister, Jan Smuts, seemed to offer the hopes of further reforms and freedom for all South African people. After the war these hopes were dashed and they simply fuelled black anger.

Many whites had become alarmed by the changes in the Africans' position which had accompanied the wartime industrial boom. Jan Smuts had not clearly rejected racial integration in the way the Nationalists had done. His United Party represented mainly English mining, and financial and industrial interests, which stood to gain from the flood of black workers to the cities. The Nationalists represented Afrikaner farmers and workers who feared they would lose out to the blacks and bitterly opposed any mixing of races. The Nationalists swept to power in the 1948 election. Their victory meant that the rigid policy of racial segregation (apartheid – the Afrikaner word for separateness) and minority white domination were entrenched in law with the full backing of the state.

△ Jan Smuts was South Africa's deputy prime minister and prime minister during the 1930s and 1940s. He led the United Party and was pro-British during the Second World War. In 1942 he announced that "segregation has fallen on evil days" and this led many Africans to expect him to reform apartheid. However, after 1945 they found this was not the case.

Apartheid

Apartheid after 1948 merely confirmed the long-standing system of controlling black workers and oppressing all blacks in South Africa. The Nationalists set out to reshape South African society for the benefit of the white "master-race", in a series of laws reminiscent of Nazism. The South African people were divided into four "racial groups" – whites, coloureds, Indians and Africans. The separation of the races and ethnic groups was decreed in every sphere of life by laws such as the Group Areas Act of 1950 and the Reservation of Separate Amenities Act of 1953. People of different colours were not even allowed to travel in the same ambulance or end their days in the same cemetery! Sex between black and white was made punishable by up to seven years' imprisonment under the 1950 Immorality Act. Blacks were also forbidden by law to do highly paid jobs.

Starting with the Suppression of Communism Act which banned the Communist Party in 1950, the government steadily gave itself more powers to silence its opponents. It also recruited more police and soldiers to enforce the new laws. This intensified repression provoked considerable black resistance. Black nationalists and socialists joined in an alliance. They now resorted to organising people on a mass basis to struggle against white domination.

△ In 1948 D F Malan and his National Party (with the smaller Afrikaner Party) won a victory for the Afrikaners in the general election. For the next 40 years the National Party dominated white politics in South Africa. After 1966 it increasingly won support from English-speaking whites. After its initial victory, the National Party introduced many of the acts which defined apartheid. It also worked to improve the Afrikaners' economic position. Afrikaners started to control the civil service, the police force, the army and other state institutions.

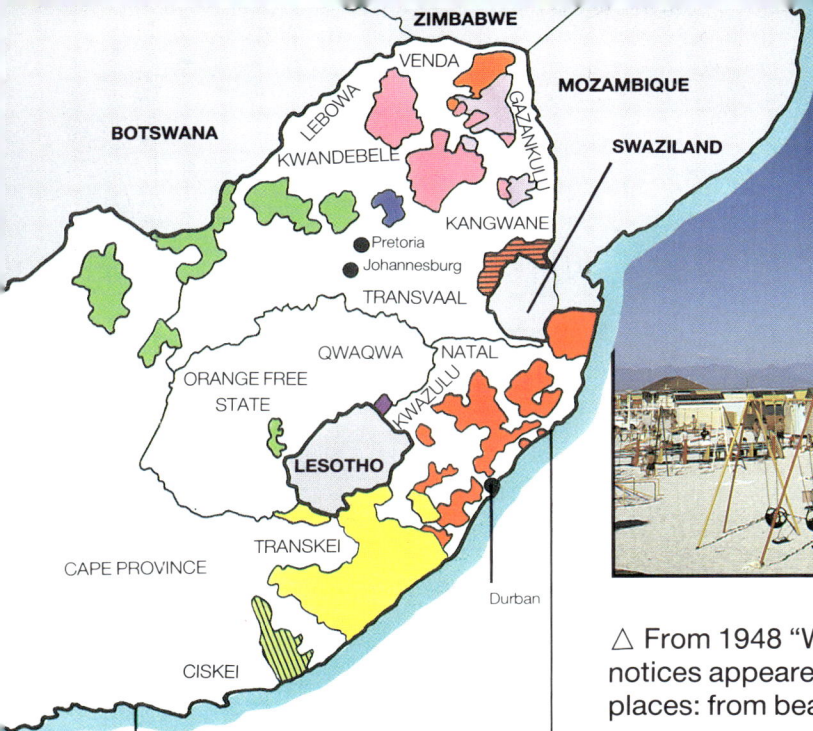

Map legend

"Independent" homelands

- ■ Bophuthatswana
- ▨ Ciskei
- ■ Transkei
- ■ Venda

Non-independent homelands

- ▤ KaNgwane
- ■ KwaZulu
- ■ Lebowa
- ■ Qwaqwa
- ■ Gazankulu
- ■ KwaNdebele

△ The map shows those parts of eastern South Africa that have been put aside as homelands for Africans. The human cost of this Bantustan policy has been enormous. At least 3.5 million people have been forcibly removed since 1960. Two million have been moved from "white" South Africa into the already over-populated Bantustans. In the 1980s, four out of five households in the Bantustans were living in poverty.

△ From 1948 "Whites Only" notices appeared in public places: from beaches, to toilets, parks, buses, restaurants, trains, hotels, cinemas and theatres.

Verwoerd and the Bantustans

Following the end of the Second World War, South Africa's racist system came under attack from other countries. India was particularly critical of the treatment of its citizens in South Africa. In response to this criticism of apartheid, the South African prime minister, Hendrik Verwoerd, launched the Bantustan policy. At the time many of the European imperial powers had promised their colonies independence. The Bantustan policy was South Africa's version of giving independence. It was intended to be the second stage of apartheid – total separation of the races. Eighty-seven per cent of South Africa was to be reserved for white control while the remaining 13 per cent was to be divided into about ten black homelands, or Bantustans. Black South Africans, the policy stated, would only have political rights and citizenship in these homelands, which would proceed to self-government and "independence". By separating the Africans into these independent homelands, the whites could then be said to be in the majority in South Africa itself.

There was, said the Nationalists, no black majority in South Africa. Instead, there were a number of different black "nations", each of which must proceed to "self-determination" in its own "homeland". The policy envisaged that Africans would be allowed to enter white South Africa only on a "temporary" basis as migrant workers, living without their families in single-sex hostels for 11 months of the year. A 1952 act then introduced passbooks, which were the documents any African living and working in town had to carry.

13

Resistance and repression

Black people responded to apartheid laws with resistance and were met with repression. After 1960 black people took up arms themselves.

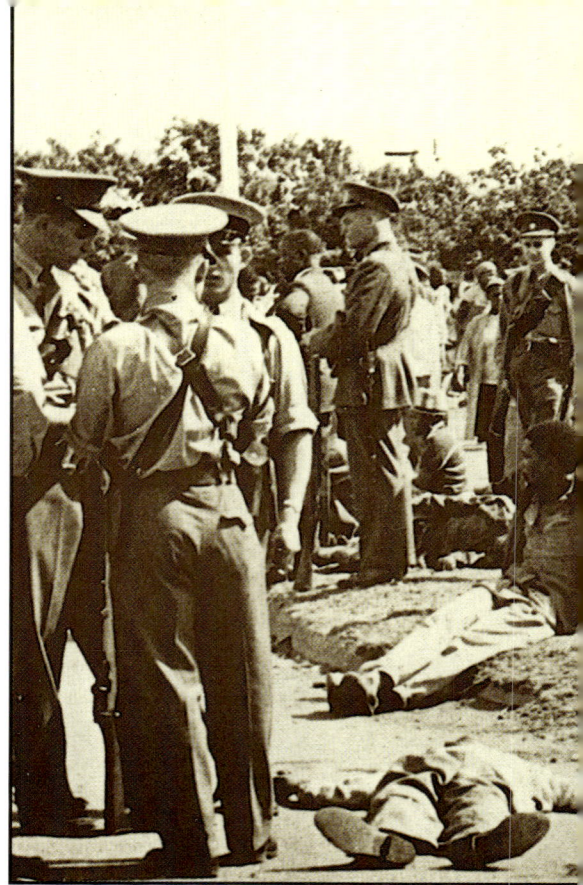

In 1943 the ANC had issued its first political programme, demanding the right to vote for everyone and a redivision of the land. In 1949 a Programme of Action, drafted by members of the Youth League, was adopted. It called for strikes, boycotts and civil disobedience. In a joint campaign with the South African Indian Congress (SAIC) in 1952, the ANC mobilised large numbers of volunteers to defy apartheid laws. Over 8,000 people were arrested. They went to prison, refusing to pay bail or fines. Early in 1953 the ANC called off the campaign.

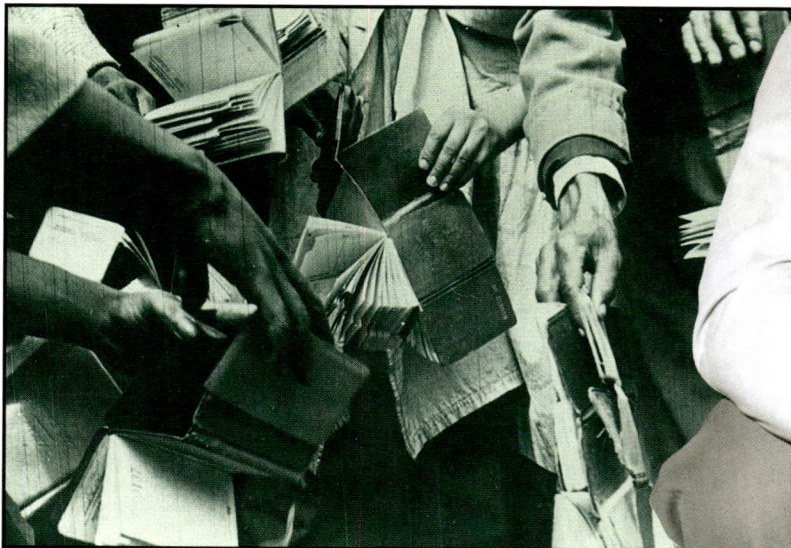

△ This was the scene after police opened fire on a demonstration outside a police station in Sharpeville, near Johannesburg, in 1960. Some 69 people died and 186 were wounded – most of them in the back as they tried to escape. This violence on the part of the police did not put an end to the demonstrations but instead led to further unrest.

◁ *Far left*: Africans burn their passbooks in protest at the pass laws in 1959. *Left*: Nelson Mandela also took part in the passbook burning protest. The South African government used the pass laws to control the movements of African people. The passbooks stated where Africans were allowed to live and work. If an African person did not have his or her passbook, he or she could be arrested.

The Congress Alliance

This defiance campaign dramatically increased support for the ANC and its allies. ANC membership rose rapidly from 7,000 to 100,000. The campaign also strengthened co-operation between the ANC and the Indian Congress. A year later the two organisations joined two other groups to form the Congress Alliance.

The ANC and its allies decided to draw up a programme for South Africa's future development. At the Congress of the People held at Kliptown in 1955, almost 3,000 delegates of all races drew up the Freedom Charter which declared that "South Africa belongs to all who live in it, black and white". It demanded democracy and the right to vote for all South Africans, and redistribution of wealth between black and white.

In December 1956, 156 Congress leaders were rounded up by the police and charged with High Treason. The Freedom Charter was said to be a "communist document". However after a trial lasting four years, not one defendant was found guilty.

Meanwhile a group of African nationalists in the ANC soon made it clear they objected to parts of the Charter and the statement that South Africa belonged to both black and white. They were unhappy with the ANC's links with the Communist Party and its alliance with white democrats. Using the slogan "Africa for the Africans", this group broke away from the ANC in 1958 to form the Pan-Africanist Congress (PAC) in 1959, with Robert Sobukwe as President.

Sharpeville

The Congress Alliance continued to organise resistance campaigns, particularly against the introduction of passbooks. They also protested against a special education system for blacks. The government did not stand idly by. Each campaign was broken by force and by the introduction of further laws.

Then on 21 March 1960, outside the Sharpeville police station, the police opened fire on an unarmed crowd of PAC supporters protesting against passbook laws, killing 69. The country erupted in demonstrations and strikes. The government announced a state of emergency and thousands were arrested. Foreign companies responded by taking their money out of the country, and the United Nations' Security Council condemned the South African government for the first time.

For South Africa, 1960 was a turning point. Previously leaders of the ANC had used non-violent resistance against the repression brought in by successive governments. Now they were prepared to take up arms in their struggle.

Sharpeville brought to an end half a century of non-violent struggle – during which time the state had used violence to protect its interests. As Mandela said "fifty years of non-violence had brought the Africans nothing". The ANC and its allies were now united over their goal – the overthrowing of apartheid – and its replacement by a non-racial, democratic state.

Bannings

The ANC and PAC were banned. The ANC sent Tambo, then deputy president, to build up support for the ANC abroad. At the same time Mandela began to organise the ANC in secret. In 1961 he became the first commander of a new armed force, *Umkhonto we Sizwe* (Spear of the Nation, also known as MK), the military wing of the ANC. This movement, together with Poqo (the military wing of the PAC) and the African Resistance Movement (made up of mainly white professionals and students), decided that violence was the only option left.

In their first 18 months *Umkhonto* carried out 200 sabotage attacks, all – at this stage – aimed at avoiding the loss of life. Their revolutionary violence was not successful, in that the security forces were soon able to smash the organisations involved.

△ In the early 1960s *Umkhonto we Sizwe* (MK) bombed post offices, government buildings and power lines.

▽ A woman protests outside the court where Nelson Mandela and other members of *Umkhonto*'s high command were on trial, accused of sabotage, in 1964.

△ Steve Biko wrote in 1971 that "Black consciousness is in essence the realisation by the black man of the need to rally together with their brothers around the cause of their subjection – the blackness of their skin – and to operate as a group in order to rid themselves of the shackles that bind them to perpetual servitude."

The police state

In August 1962 Mandela was captured and in mid-1964 he and his comrades were sentenced to life imprisonment. The police used torture and new detention laws to smash the ANC's secret organisation. Thousands of activists were imprisoned or driven into exile. Large numbers of PAC members were also arrested and the PAC was virtually destroyed as an organised force. In 1963 the first detainee died in detention at the hands of the security police. Looksmart Ngudle was said to have "committed suicide by hanging". More deaths followed.

By the mid-1960s the government was firmly in control and foreign companies began to invest their money in South Africa again. They knew they could make large profits on their investments because black workers were paid such low wages. The South African economy enjoyed rapid growth and the living standards of whites rose.

In 1966 John Vorster became the new prime minister. He had already served as a Minister of Police and was known to have pro-Nazi sympathies. As prime minister he presided over what was for black people a rule of terror. Many opponents of apartheid were taken into detention and tortured. Those who survived and were released were often placed under house arrest.

Black Consciousness

Exiled ANC guerrillas tried, unsuccessfully, to fight their way back home during 1967-68 from Rhodesia (now called Zimbabwe). However in the early 1970s a wave of resistance surfaced inside South Africa. A new generation of black activists, who had grown up under the repression, emerged. They wanted to assert black unity and dignity, and by the mid-1970s had formed several new organisations, known as the Black Consciousness Movement. There was growing awareness of the evils of apartheid. Books, poetry and pamphlets now publicly talked of the detention and torture. A booming economy meant that Africans were taking semi-skilled jobs and this led to the re-establishment of black trade unions. A number of ANC former political prisoners also began to organise underground ANC cells within the country. Most importantly the attempts to control black education backfired. Steve Biko became leader of the South African Students Organisation, which was part of the Black Consciousness Movement. As in the past, the apartheid state responded by jailing and banning the leaders.

The Soweto Uprising

When school students in the huge black township of Soweto (Southwest Township), outside Johannesburg, marched in protest against government changes in their education system on 16 June 1976, they were gunned down by the police. Black anger exploded. What followed was an uprising against apartheid on an unprecedented scale, led by youths. Over several months of street demonstrations and rioting, all the strands of anti-apartheid resistance became involved.

The South African government responded with considerable brutality, killing several hundred school children by the end of 1977, and enraging the international community in the process. World opinion was also shocked when the news came out that the most prominent advocate of Black Consciousness, Steve Biko, had died in detention at the hands of the security forces.

During the late 1970s students continued to protest against apartheid. Community-based organisations (civics) opposed rent increases and built up support in the townships. Women and young people formed their own groups, and non-racial unions continued to grow in numbers. All these organisations were united in their opposition to the government.

Abroad, in the United States and Western Europe, the campaign for economic sanctions against South Africa, initiated by the ANC and local anti-apartheid movements, at last began to meet with some success. Many people began to put pressure on their governments to stop trading with and investing in companies in South Africa.

Exodus of the young

Meanwhile thousands of young people had left South Africa after June 1976. Many wanted military training as guerrillas. The vast majority of them went into the ANC's military wing, and *Umkhonto*'s armed activities increased significantly and steadily from then on. This coincided with the liberation of Mozambique and Angola from Portuguese colonial rule in 1975.

The independence of Mozambique presented a threat to the white government in Rhodesia, which had relied on Mozambique's ports for its oil supplies. In 1978 Rhodesia came under pressure from African guerrillas fighting for independence. Mozambican independence also helped the ANC's armed struggle as it could establish transit routes to South Africa through Mozambican territory.

△ In 1976 thousands of black school students in Soweto protested when the government insisted that they should be taught half of their lessons in Afrikaans. They did not want to learn the language of the people who were oppressing them. There were nationwide demonstrations and the government reacted brutally.

▷ This was the first victim of the Soweto Uprising: the 13-year old Hector Peterson. An official enquiry into the uprising estimated that at least 575 people were killed, of whom 134 were under 18. Anti-apartheid activists said the figure was much higher.

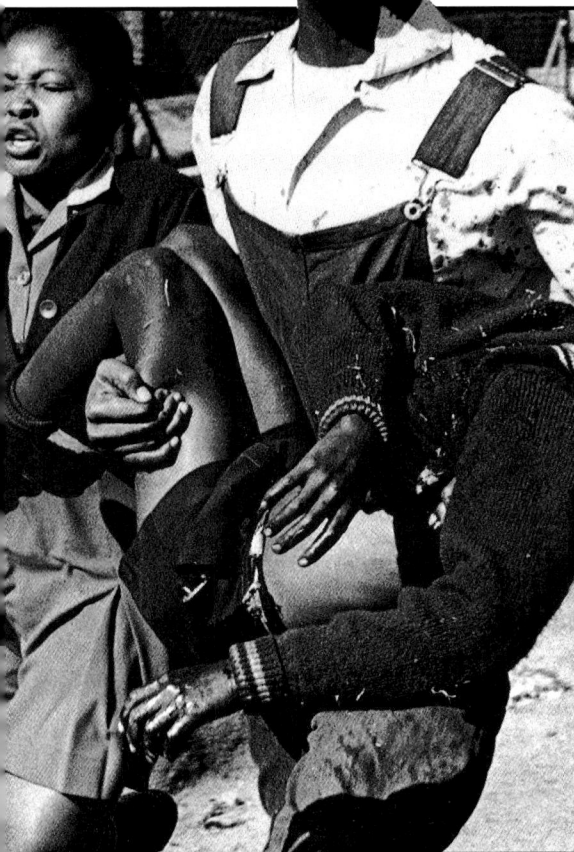

The changing position of the Afrikaners

After Soweto the ruling National Party was split over how to cope with the new situation. There had been many economic changes, which all influenced government policy. First, the South African economy had been transformed so that it was dominated by a handful of large companies. By 1978 four companies controlled 80 per cent of the share capital (that is, they controlled many smaller companies by owning their shares). The largest, the Anglo-American Corporation, controlled 55 per cent. Secondly, Afrikaners had used political power to advance their "own people" economically. As a result, there had been many changes in Afrikaner society. The number of Afrikaners in the professions (teaching, medical, legal and others) trebled in three decades. Some Afrikaner companies became very powerful, and they developed links with large English companies. The Nationalists had also built up a huge state-controlled business sector.

In 1978 the minister of defence, P W Botha, took over as head of government from Vorster. This represented a victory for the faction in the ruling National Party which was backed by Afrikaner big business, who favoured limited reform to apartheid because they were afraid of instability. Botha's aim was to sacrifice some of apartheid, such as keeping better paid jobs reserved for whites, in order to ensure the long-term survival of the system. Botha's background in the army led him to rely on the army and the police for advice.

"Total Strategy" to meet the "total onslaught"

In the same year, "Total National Strategy" was adopted as official policy in order to counter what was seen as a "communist-inspired total onslaught" against South Africa. This onslaught was said to come from the neighbouring countries who had banded together to form the Frontline States (Angola, Mozambique, Botswana, Zambia and others). It also came from the ANC and the Namibian liberation movement, known as the South-West Africa People's Organisation (SWAPO). It even came from the United Nations, the Organisation of African Unity and the West! The regime was convinced that apartheid could be defended by using the army against enemies abroad and by making a few reforms and using force to knock out its critics at home.

The SADCC

Botha wanted to build what he called a constellation of Southern African states, dominated by South Africa. He also wanted South Africa's neighbouring states to be tied to it by economic and security agreements. These countries could provide much-needed markets for South Africa's exports as well as new business opportunities.

In response black-ruled neighbouring states formed the Southern Africa Development Co-ordinating Conference (SADCC) after Rhodesia became independent Zimbabwe in 1980. SADCC wanted to reduce economic ties with South Africa: many of the neighbouring states depended on rail links through South Africa to get imports. They also depended on the wages of their citizens working in South African mines. The giant Anglo-American Corporation of South Africa and its associated companies had trading interests in Botswana, Zimbabwe, Zambia and Namibia.

Destabilisation

Throughout the period after the Soweto uprising, South Africa practised a policy towards its neighbours of "destabilisation". This meant direct military intervention by South African troops, or the training and support of local opposition groups to provoke civil war within these countries and fight as proxies on its behalf.

South Africa also wanted to make its neighbours stop ANC guerrillas from returning to South Africa itself through their territories. All the countries of the region, except for Tanzania and Malawi, experienced direct military attack by South Africa. South Africa also supported local opposition groups, such as the Mozambique National Resistance (MNR) and the Union for the Total Independence of Angola (UNITA). Both the Mozambican and Angolan peoples have endured terrible suffering as a result of these wars. Between 1980-88 some 325,000 Mozambicans and Angolans died because of the wars in their countries. By 1989 half of Mozambique's population had had to leave their homes.

Towards the end of the 1980s South Africa changed its policy and started an economic and political offensive to dominate the region. This change occurred after South Africa's military setback at the hands of the joint Cuban/Angolan forces at the Battle of Cuito Cunavale in 1987-88. This defeat forced the South Africans to withdraw their troops from Angola and Namibia which South Africa had occupied for decades in defiance of the United Nations.

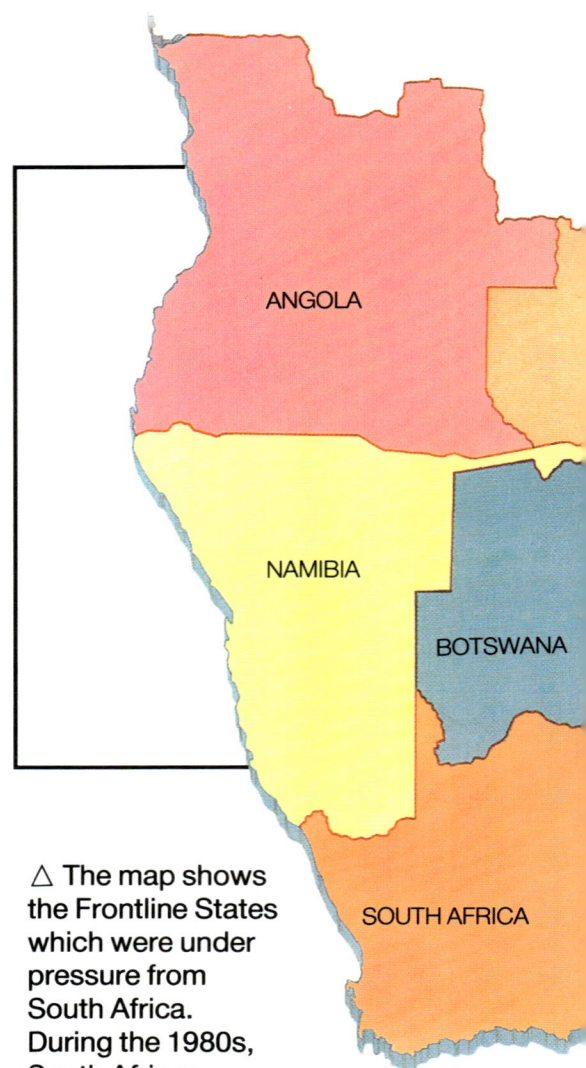

△ The map shows the Frontline States which were under pressure from South Africa. During the 1980s, South African troops undertook raids on all the neighbouring countries.

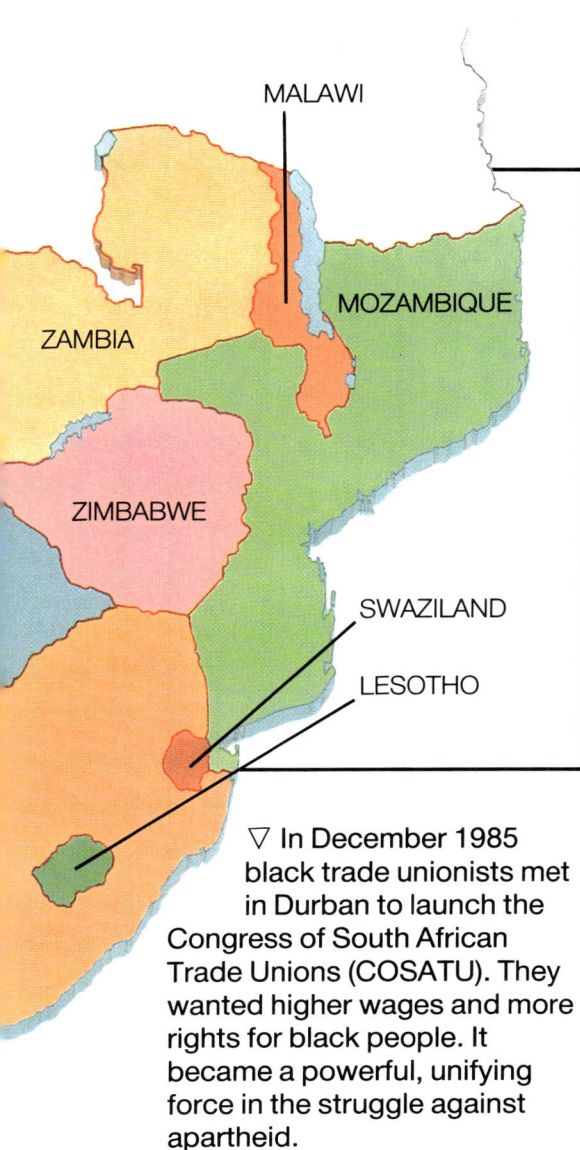

MALAWI
MOZAMBIQUE
ZAMBIA
ZIMBABWE
SWAZILAND
LESOTHO

▽ In December 1985 black trade unionists met in Durban to launch the Congress of South African Trade Unions (COSATU). They wanted higher wages and more rights for black people. It became a powerful, unifying force in the struggle against apartheid.

By then South Africa had successfully destabilised its neighbours. Most countries in the region had been forced to restrict the ANC presence and some had accepted economic co-operation on South Africa's terms. The proxy groups, such as the MNR and UNITA, had become less dependent on South African support and were now able to sustain themselves by plundering Mozambique, Angola and Zimbabwe.

Attempts at constitutional reforms

Meanwhile the situation in South Africa had also become less stable. Since 1977 the Nationalists had talked of introducing a new constitution. This was an attempt to divide the Indian and coloured people from the African majority by giving them some political power in their own elected bodies (known as chambers). There were to be three chambers: for whites, for Indians and for coloureds but the white chamber had ultimate power.

A multiracial cabinet, drawn from the three chambers, was responsible for general affairs. Ministers' councils from each chamber looked after "own affairs", such as education, health and local government. The state president was elected by a college of members of parliament and it was he who decided which affairs were general or own. It was a very cumbersome and expensive system of government, which left out the Africans.

In 1983 a United Democratic Front (UDF) had been established to co-ordinate resistance to the new constitution. The front brought together one and a half million people in hundreds of groups which had formed after the Soweto Uprising. The new constitution was introduced in October 1984 but it failed because black people refused to co-operate.

The UDF campaign for a boycott of elections to the chambers in 1984 was a great success: only 17.5 per cent of the coloured electorate voted, and 16.6 per cent of the Indians. A similar boycott campaign against elections for black local authorities, considered "puppet" pro-apartheid bodies by the ANC, in the African townships in 1983 had resulted in an average poll of only 10 per cent.

In December 1985 the Congress of South African Trade Unions (COSATU) was launched. It was the largest federation of workers in South African history. The alliance between the UDF and COSATU, both ANC-aligned, became known eventually as the Mass Democratic Movement (MDM).

The 1984-86 Uprising

Long-standing black grievances over housing and education and the government's attempt to impose its new constitution sparked off the most serious challenge yet to minority rule. The spontaneous uprising, which started in September 1984, followed a call from the ANC to its followers to make the country ungovernable by destroying the state administration in black townships and the Bantustans. Black township councillors and black policemen were the major targets of black anger. Some workers refused to go to work, students refused to attend classes and there were many demonstrations.

The South African government responded by imposing successive states of emergency. The government also began to use more "informal" methods of repression. Death squads and black vigilantes (self-appointed police) appeared in the second half of 1985. Their targets were anti-apartheid activists. In 1989 former death squad agents admitted that their activities were organised by the state. Vigilantes were organised by black councillors and Bantustan officials and in some cases were directly assisted by the police. By the late 1980s almost every township and factory in the country was involved, but by 1987-88 the South African government had crushed the uprising.

△ Crowds fight in the streets of Sharpeville in 1984. During the 1984-86 Uprising the police intervened to protect black township councillors from attack. They were seen as servants of apartheid.

International pressure

After 1985 many Western banks and companies took their money out of South Africa and this deepened the economic crisis. South Africa's currency, the Rand, lost value and prices began to climb as inflation got higher. South Africa no longer had the means to fight foreign wars.

In 1985 there were major changes in international affairs. The new Soviet leader, Mikhail Gorbachev, launched a major reform programme. Relations between East and West gradually improved and this changed the international situation. The United States and the Soviets began to co-operate in the search for solutions to regional conflicts. The Soviet Union became increasingly preoccupied with its own economic crisis and other problems, and less willing and able to fund the foreign wars like those in Southern Africa.

The major Western powers also began to move away from seeing South Africa as their main ally in southern Africa. South Africa was no longer the bastion against communism. The Western powers also had to consider their wider interests. In particular, Britain began to worry that if there was a revolt in South Africa, its companies would lose a lot of money. In 1986 the United States passed an anti-apartheid act which included many economic sanctions, such as, ending new investments in and bank loans to South Africa. The European Community also imposed sanctions.

▽ As more and more people died at the hands of the police during the 1980s, funerals became important ceremonies. This is the funeral of Pedro Page, who died in September 1989.

The State of Emergency 1986-1989

Although there had been several states of emergency before, none compared to the one introduced in 1986. It was nationwide and for an indefinite period. Media coverage was virtually forbidden, hundreds of anti-apartheid activists were arrested and the security forces unleashed an unprecedented wave of brutality.

Since 1985 some influential whites had begun to say that eventually Africans in South Africa would gain a share of the political power. Sanctions were biting and South Africa was becoming increasingly isolated in the world community. It was time for the government to talk with the ANC and other African organisations. As the 1980s ended, the apartheid state faced a severe and chronic political and economic crisis. Internal unrest would probably return in ever-greater intensity, and the international economic and diplomatic price of putting it down in the usual ways was too high. A new approach was needed.

Dismantling apartheid

In 1989 and 1990 the South African president announced some changes in apartheid laws. A few political prisoners were freed, but does this mean an end to apartheid?

De Klerk's mandate for reforms

During 1989 the black movement maintained its pressure on the South African government and launched a well-publicised defiance campaign against apartheid and emergency laws. Hundreds of political prisoners went on hunger strike, many securing their release. ANC and SACP flags were openly displayed in defiance of relevant laws.

In 1989, Frederik Willem de Klerk took over the leadership, first of the ruling party and then of the government, before the September elections for the white-controlled parliament. On the night after the voting for three chambers, the police killed over 20 people who were protesting about the elections. Elections to the coloured and Indian houses of parliament had been boycotted, and three million black workers and students had stayed away from work and school in a dramatic demonstration of black opinion.

De Klerk announced that the election results had been a 70 per cent mandate for change by putting the National and Democratic Party vote together. In fact, the Conservative Party had made great gains, advocating a tougher pro-apartheid policy. It replaced the Democrats as the main white opposition and gained many votes in the small, rural towns and among white workers. The Nationalists were moving to the centre of South African politics and still had predominantly Afrikaner membership. But they were now more representative of South African business interests as a whole.

Unbanning the banned organisations

The following month de Klerk released seven of Mandela's closest colleagues from prison, and allowed rallies to welcome them. On 2 February 1990 he lifted the bans on the ANC, PAC, SACP and other organisations and invited them to join him in seeking a negotiated settlement to the conflict. Mandela himself was released within weeks.

The euphoria in the black community which greeted his release confirmed the ANC's overwhelming popularity. The ANC began to organise this support and at the same time entered into pre-negotiation talks with the government. The KwaZulu Bantustan leader, Gatsha Buthelezi, considered himself the leader of South Africa's seven million Zulus and he became angry at being left out of negotiations. His organisation, Inkatha, had some support in the Bantustans but not in the cities.

Inkatha violence

Inkatha vigilante violence was stepped up, first in Natal and then, from August, in the Transvaal townships, where hostels housing migrant Zulu workers were used as bases for attacks on neighbouring communities. The attacks in the Transvaal coincided with the ANC's suspension of the armed struggle on 6 August. However, ANC supporters immediately asked the ANC to supply weapons to defend themselves from Inkatha. Over 700 people were killed in the Transvaal in August and September. The ANC has strong support traditionally among Xhosa speakers but draws its membership from all of South Africa's people. The conflict in Natal has been mainly between Inkatha and ANC supporters, who are all Zulu speakers.

The Transvaal violence (and the continuing war in Natal) has put a terrible strain on relations between Mandela and de Klerk. The ANC accused the government of talking peace while waging war against the organisation. Mandela declared that there was a "hidden hand" behind the violence: elements of the security forces and other right-wing white extremists.

There was widespread evidence of police collusion with Inkatha. Yet de Klerk defended the "even handedness" of the police and imposed an "Iron Fist" security clampdown in the townships, supposedly to stop the violence but in the eyes of many actually aimed at anti-apartheid activists. By mid-October the ANC was accusing de Klerk and his ministers of undermining the peace process.

△ In February 1990 the ANC leader, Nelson Mandela, was freed after 27 years in jail. During his time in custody, the ANC had demanded his release. By the 1980s many world leaders had put pressure on the South African government to release him.

◁ In 1989 F W de Klerk became the new president of South Africa. He was the leader of the National Party, which was losing support among the Afrikaners. During 1989 and 1990 he announced some changes in apartheid laws and freed a few long-term political prisoners.

International pressure for reforms

In general the position of the international organisations, such as the European Community, the United Nations and other bodies, has been that sanctions should continue until there is evidence of irreversible change in South Africa. Specific preconditions have also been laid down, such as the release of prisoners and the end of emergency rule, as well as the repeal of apartheid laws.

De Klerk's government has not really met these preconditions. De Klerk lifted the state of emergency, but retained the Internal Security Act which gives the police almost unlimited powers. As far as apartheid laws go, he has given notice that the Group Areas Act and the Natives Land Acts will be repealed during 1991. There is no talk of the Population Registration Act going, so for the time being people will still be classified according to the colour of their skin.

In October 1990 the Separate Amenities Act was abolished. This should have opened public facilities to everyone but high prices and local laws will ensure that many swimming baths, libraries, schools, hospitals and other institutions remain for whites only. The major "petty apartheid" laws may have gone, but there remains much public separation and inequality.

▽ In August 1990 Inkatha supporters attacked residents in the Soweto township, outside Johannesburg. The government sent in troops to stop the fighting, but was accused by the ANC of bias to Inkatha.

◁ Gold and diamonds are the basis of South Africa's wealth. Most mineworkers are black yet white people own the companies that exploit the mines. The companies need the 500,000 mineworkers, who are beginning to get higher rates of pay for the dangerous work they do. The mining companies want stability in South Africa so they can continue in business. The ANC has said it would consider bringing the mines under state control.

▽ In 1990 President de Klerk flew to Washington to meet the US President George Bush. It was the first meeting between leaders from the two countries for over 40 years. Bush gave de Klerk a warm reception, which boosted his standing.

Another point raised by anti-apartheid campaigners is that repealing apartheid laws is not enough. Removing the restrictions on Africans' rights to buy land in "white" South Africa is meaningless to the rural poor who have no money to buy land, let alone farm it.

By October 1990 only a few political prisoners had been released and a few exiles had been allowed to return home. One ANC executive member, Mac Maharaj, was in hospital after being assaulted by police in detention.

International response to the reforms

In October 1990 de Klerk visited the United States for the first time as president. President George Bush immediately declared that the changes in South Africa were "irreversible" and that sanctions should be lifted. However, a move to lift sanctions as soon as possible was curbed by Congress, the US parliament, which did not agree with Bush's interpretation of events. The British prime minister, Margaret Thatcher, was also in a tremendous rush to lift sanctions and to persuade the European Community to do the same. Meanwhile, the major Western powers have been courting Mandela and the ANC, determined to ensure that the process towards a multiracial democratic society becomes a reality.

A post-apartheid South Africa

The ANC has declared that a post-apartheid South Africa must be based on a fairer distribution of wealth. The gap between rich and poor in South Africa is wider than in any other country for which such statistics are available. Some five per cent of the population own 88 per cent of the wealth, while over half of all households have incomes below the poverty line. How far will de Klerk go with abolishing apartheid? He promised President Bush that there would never again be an all-white election. In any case he might well lose an election to the Conservatives. On the other hand, he has rejected the ANC's call for free elections to an assembly, which would draw up a constitution for a new South Africa. Instead many believe he is trying to negotiate a constitution on his own terms, which would preserve much white power.

Anti-apartheid activists

The South African army, police and unofficial agents of repression – the vigilantes and the death squads – are still largely intact and active against anti-apartheid activists. Tough treatment of political prisoners and shooting of demonstrators have continued under de Klerk, many allege with no serious attempt on his part to stop them.

If a majority government were elected, it might face the possibility of a coup. Disaffected white right-wingers might also launch a terrorist war and fight a proxy war through black vigilantes.

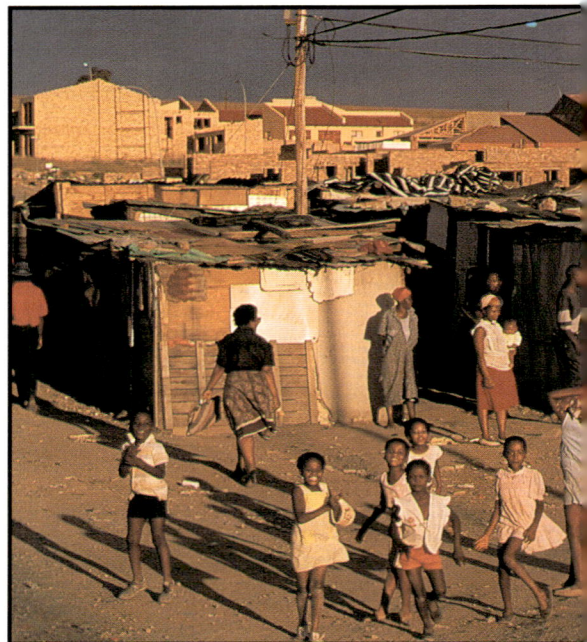

△ This is the Alexandra township. Most of the townships have poor quality houses and inadequate sewage facilities.

▽ South Africa is a country of great natural beauty. This is Camps Bay near Cape Town, where the first Dutch settlers lived.

△ Tourism is an important source of income in South Africa. Recently the number of visitors has dropped because of the unrest.

Majority rule

Apart from this disastrous security situation which a democratic government stands to inherit, there are the other aspects of apartheid's legacy which will make any government's task daunting: seven million homeless, six million unemployed, poverty on a massive scale, extreme inequality between black and white, and the ethnic and other social tensions which have in some cases been deliberately created under minority rule.

The winning of majority rule will be only the first step on a very long and hazardous road for those who want to create a democratic, united and non-racial South Africa, with a more just distribution of wealth. But that first step will still mark a great advance, not only for the people of South Africa but for the entire region. It will stop the devastating regional wars and integrate South Africa's rich economic potential into the regional economy. It will also remove what has come to be recognised by the international community as a major threat to world peace.

The end of apartheid?

When announcing his reforms de Klerk indicated that he intended to maintain white ascendancy in South Africa. He said "We want to build a new South Africa in which all people will participate in decisions affecting their lives and at all tiers of government, but," he added, "in such a way that no one group will be in a position to dominate others". There are doubts as to whether this promises a fully, democratic government structure with voting rights for all people irrespective of colour and race.

Today the whites in South Africa must recognise that by the year 2005 they will form a mere 10 per cent of the population. Not all Africans, coloureds and Indians are poorly paid, some have reached higher levels of management and the professions. The economy is suffering not only from the effect of international sanctions and high inflation, but also from the huge cost of administering the apartheid system.

The initial reforms have been welcomed as a step in the right direction, but they do not yet go so far as removing apartheid in South Africa. Many people think the Nationalists are still trying to maintain the status quo. The prospect of a civil war in the townships and the threat posed by right-wing extremists, however, mean that the South African people must urgently find a way of securing a peaceful end to apartheid.

South Africa facts

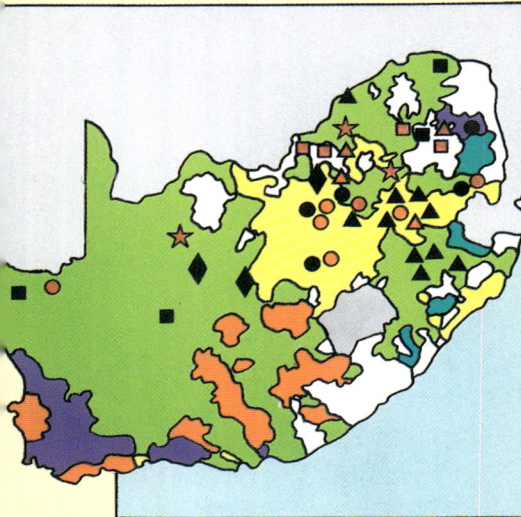

Cereals

Forestry

Fruit

Livestock

Wool

No data

○ Silver

● Gold

◆ Diamonds

▲ Coal

★ Iron

△ Platinum

▣ Chromium

◼ Copper

△ South Africa is more or less self-sufficient in minerals and agricultural products except for wheat. It exports many raw materials, including coal, steel and iron as well as gold and diamonds. However, it has to import oil and is vulnerable to oil sanctions, which were first imposed by the Organisation of Petroleum Exporting Countries in 1973. It also needs to import heavy machinery for factories, electronic equipment and trucks. So international trade is important.

Population: 36,005,000 of whom 27,000,000 are Africans (75 per cent), 4,950,000 are whites (13 per cent), 3,127,000 (9 per cent) are coloureds and 928,000 (3 per cent) are Indian.

Capitals: Pretoria is the seat of government; Cape Town the legislative capital; and Bloemfontein is the judicial capital.

Major products: Gold, diamonds, fruit and vegetables.

Mining

For every tonne of gold mined in South Africa, one worker dies and 17 are seriously injured. Since the beginning of the century about 50,000 gold miners have been killed, most of them black. The pay increase given to white miners in 1990 was worth ten times that offered to black miners.

Minerals account for two-thirds of South Africa's export earnings. It has over 40 valuable minerals. South Africa is the main producer of gold, chromite and platinum in the world, second in manganese, third in uranium, fourth in antimony and fifth in diamonds.

Environment

The environmental Worldwatch Institute recently condemned South Africa for creating "ecological wastelands" in the Bantustans. The damage was caused by excessive mining and overdependence on polluting sources of energy, mainly coal. (As a result, South African whites are contributing more than any other group on earth to global warming through the greenhouse effect: a white

South African generates nine tonnes of carbon dioxide annually compared to five tonnes per person in the United States and a world average of one tonne.)

Human rights

By May 1989 over 50,000 people had been detained under the successive States of Emergency, 15,000 of whom were under the age of 18.

On 30 August 1990, the Human Rights Commission reported that there were 3,000 political prisoners, over 200 political trials in process and 58 political prisoners on death row.

Economy

Rising oil costs because of the Gulf crisis are putting the balance of payments under pressure and are likely to push inflation above the present official level of 13.3 per cent.

South Africa's unemployment rate is 30 per cent and rising. The gap between rich and poor in South Africa is enormous. Whites own 87 per cent of the land and 95 per cent of industry. The richest five per cent of the population own 88 per cent of all personally owned wealth.

Bantustans

The 10 Bantustans make up 13.7 per cent of the land area of the country, yet they accommodate more than half (57 per cent or 20 million) of South Africa's population. They account for three per cent of the annual production of the country. They are largely destitute of resources and acutely short of land. A number of the homelands are like scattered puzzle pieces.

KwaZulu, for example, consists of 40 pieces of land throughout Natal province (see map on page 13). The South African government regards homeland citizens as aliens.

In the 1980s, four out of five Bantustan households were living in poverty. The figure for the rest of South Africa was one in two. More than a million people are without homes. One in two adults are unemployed, making up the vast bulk of South Africa's total unemployment figure of about six million. Black infant mortality, in the Bantustans, is 10 times higher than for white children (120 per 1,000 live births as opposed to 12).

Health care
Baragwanath Hospital outside Johannesburg serves four million black people and is so crowded that patients have often had to share beds or sleep on the floor. Meanwhile in the nearby Johannesburg General Hospital for whites, half the beds have often been empty. There are 14 different health Ministries for 14 different apartheid-defined population groups! But hospitals were desegregated in 1990.

Education
Some 80 per cent of black schools have no electric power for heating or lighting. The government estimates it would take £1,300 million to bring black schools up to the level of white schools in terms of resources – it has offered £200 million at present. The National Education Co-ordinating Committee's own estimate is six times the government figure. In 1989 the government abandoned a ten-year plan to upgrade black education to the white level, saying it had insufficient funds.

Urbanisation
South Africa has the world's fastest rate of urbanisation. Some 80 per cent of the black population will be living in the cities by the year 2020. Blacks already account for two-thirds of trade in central Johannesburg. Black consumers are increasingly important.

▽ Migrant workers in a hostel. The system of migrant workers persists to this day. Although most gold miners are South Africans at least 200,000 come from outside South Africa. Many come from Lesotho, Mozambique, Botswana, Swaziland and elsewhere.

Parties and groups

National Party (NP)
It has been the ruling party since 1948. It was led by Dr Verwoerd, B J Vorster and P W Botha from 1958 to 1989. F W de Klerk was elected leader in 1989. It has seen numerous splits on the right in recent years. It recently opened its doors to all races but with certain restrictions. So far only a few blacks have shown signs of wanting to join.

Democratic Party
Now led by Zac de Beer of the huge Anglo-American Corporation, after a leadership struggle following the merger of three liberal parties to form the Democratic Party. It is the party of English and some Afrikaner big business. It has lost its relevance since de Klerk moved to the centre of South African politics. It is currently debating whether to ally itself with the ANC or the National Party.

Conservative Party (CP) led by
Andries Treurnicht who was expelled together with other ultra-right MPs from the National Party in 1982. The CP has a strong base among the police, farmers and white workers, who are predominantly Afrikaners. In the 1989 elections it became the official opposition in parliament. The CP has increasingly begun to co-operate with more militant neo-Nazi groups like the para-military **Afrikaner Weerstandsbeweging (AWB)** (led by Eugene Terre'Blanche) whose official emblem resembles a swastika. Some estimates put the number of white fascist groups as high as 46. Eugene Terre'Blanche says there are eight main organisations.

Increasingly the Afrikaner extreme right is moving towards the idea of an independent Boer state. However, in 1990 the Afrikaner extreme right seems to be in disarray.

Dr Hendrik Verwoerd

△ Eugene Terre' Blanche addresses an AWB rally in 1990.

Archbishop Desmond Tutu

Jay Naidoo of COSATU

Chief Gatsha Buthelezi

South African churches
While ANC and PAC leaders were in prison, in exile or banned, church leaders became prominent in the fight against apartheid. Desmond Tutu, the Anglican Archbishop of Cape Town, became very outspoken and was awarded the Nobel Peace Prize in 1984. Other church critics of apartheid include Allan Boesak and Frank Chikane.

African National Congress (ANC) Formed in 1912, it is the oldest and most popular organisation in the black community, and has a growing white membership. It was banned from 1960 to 1990, when talks began with the South African government. Its military wing, *Umkhonto we Sizwe* (Spear of the Nation), is observing a ceasefire in the guerrilla war it has been waging since 1961. President Oliver Tambo is recovering from a stroke. Nelson Mandela was made Deputy President in 1990.

Pan-Africanist Congress (PAC) It formed in 1959 as a split from the ANC. It was banned in 1960 and recognised by the OAU and UN as the second liberation movement of South Africa. It was unbanned on 2 February 1990. Its General Secretary is Benny Alexander.

South African Communist Party (SACP) It was formed in 1921 from the left wing of the white labour movement. By the late 1920s it was mainly African in membership and was the first organisation to call for a black republic. It was banned in 1950. It set up *Umkhonto we Sizwe* with the ANC in 1961. It was unbanned on 2 February 1990. Its General Secretary is Joe Slovo, who also sits on the ANC's executive.

United Democratic Front (UDF) It was formed in 1983 to fight P W Botha's new constitution aimed at co-opting the Indian and coloured South Africans. It is an ANC-aligned front of student, youth, women's and other anti-apartheid groups. Together with the giant **Congress of South African Trade Unions**

(COSATU), it is the main constituent of an informal alliance known as the **Mass Democratic Movement (MDM)**. A prominent UDF leader is Popo Molefe. Other COSATU figures include General Secretary Jay Naidoo and President Elijah Barayi.

Bantustans
KwaZulu is led by Chief Gatsha Buthelezi who is president of the **Inkatha Freedom Party**. Apart from Buthelezi and Lucas Mangope of Bophuthatswana, the ANC has met with considerable success in winning the Bantustan leaders to its side in support of a united, non-racial South Africa. KaNgwane's Enos Mabuza is a strong ally of the ANC, as is Major General Bantu Holomisa of the Transkei. The position of Brigadier Oupa Gqoza, who recently came to power in a coup against dictator Lennox Sebe in the Ciskei, is less clear cut. A growing number of traditional leaders have joined the ANC-aligned Congress of Traditional Leaders of South Africa (CONTRALESA).

Chronology

1652 AD The Dutch start a settlement at the Cape of Good Hope.

1795 Britain takes the Cape Colony from the Dutch.

1803 The Dutch regain the Cape Colony by treaty.

1805 The British reconquer the Cape Colony.

1816-28 The Zulu kingdom is created.

1820 British settlers arrive in the Cape Colony.

1834-35 The British defeat the Xhosa.

1835-40 The Boers leave the Cape Colony in the Great Trek.

1843 Britain annexes Natal.

1846-47 The British defeat the Xhosa again.

1852 Britain recognises the Transvaal as an independent Boer republic.

1854 Britain recognises the Orange Free State.

1867 Diamond mining begins.

1868 Britain annexes Lesotho.

1879 British forces defeat the Zulus after having been defeated at Isandhlwana.

1886 Gold mining begins on the Witwatersrand.

1899-1902 The Boer War leads to Britain conquering the Boer republics.

1910 The Cape Colony, Natal, Transvaal and the Orange Free State form the Union of South Africa.

1912 The South African Native National Congress is formed. It later becomes the African National Congress (ANC).

1913 Land Act sets aside a small amount of land for black people.

1914-18 South Africa takes part in the First World War.

1921 The South African Communist Party is set up.

1922 White miners go on strike but are put down by government forces.

1939-45 South Africa takes part in the Second World War.

1948 Afrikaner Nationalists win the general election. They begin to set up apartheid.

1950 The Population Registration Act classifies people by race; the Group Areas Act divides South Africa into zones for all the races.

1952 The ANC and its allies launch a passive resistance campaign.

1955 The Congress of the People adopts the Freedom Charter.

1956 Congress Alliance leaders are arrested for treason but are later found not guilty.

1958 Dr Verwoerd becomes prime minister.

1959 The Pan-Africanist Congress is set up.

1960 Police shoot 69 demonstrators at Sharpeville.

1964 Nelson Mandela and other ANC and PAC leaders are given life sentences.

1966-68 Lesotho, Botswana and Swaziland become independent.

1975 Mozambique and Angola gain their independence.

1976-77 Mass protests in South African townships lead to hundreds of deaths. Steve Biko is murdered.

1978 P W Botha becomes prime minister.

1980 Rhodesia becomes independent as Zimbabwe.

1981-88 South African forces invade Angola and make raids on Lesotho, Mozambique, Zimbabwe and Zambia.

1984 A new constitution gives Asians and coloureds the right to vote for their own chambers.

1984-86 Nationwide uprising against apartheid.

1986 The government declares a state of emergency, detains thousands of people and puts strict controls on media coverage of events.

1989 De Klerk succeeds Botha.

1990 Mandela is released; violence in South African townships between blacks.

Glossary

Afrikaner A white South African of mainly Dutch descent. The Afrikaans language evolved from Dutch.

Apartheid is the Afrikaans word for separateness. It is used to describe the system of laws which ensures that whites and non-whites are kept apart.

Asian A classification under the Population Registration Act of 1950. It refers to communities originating from Asian countries like India and China but excluding the Cape Malay community which is classified coloured.

Bantu Until the 1976 uprising the official apartheid term for African. Since then the official term has been black (although anti-apartheid activists prefer to use black more widely to denote all the oppressed national groups).

Boer Dutch or Afrikaans word for farmer. It came to be applied to the Dutch settlers or Afrikaners as a group.

Coloured An apartheid term for those officially classified as being of mixed descent, as well as descendants of the Khoikhoi and San (original inhabitants of the Cape) and the slaves of the Cape Colony.

Communism is the belief that all factories, land and mines should be owned by the state on behalf of all the people. In practice, the state decides who has money and fixes prices.

Democracy is a political system where everyone has the right to vote. In elections a number of parties stand which represent different interests and points of view.

English White South Africans who have the English language as their mother tongue. They are mainly descended from British settlers, or are immigrants from various countries who are classified "white" and speak English.

First World War It was fought from 1914-18. Britain, France, Russia and later Italy and the United States fought Germany, Austria-Hungary and Turkey. As a member of the British empire, South Africa took part.

Group Areas Segregated zones in towns and cities for occupation and business purposes for the white, coloured or Asian groups under the Group Areas Act of 1950. Forced removals of communities have taken place on a large scale to move residents of the "wrong" colour.

Homelands An apartheid term for the original native reserves now called Bantustans or national states, intended to imply that the "citizens" of the Bantustans originate from there.

Indian Apartheid term for the descendants of Indian citizens, many of whom arrived in the 19th century.

Nationalism This is the belief that individual communities or cultures – usually defined by a common language – should be independent.

Nazism stands for National Socialism and it was the racial doctrine put forward by Hitler in Germany in the 1920s. It was a mixture of nationalism and socialism: Hitler promised to make Germany great again and he also said he would look after the workers. He was a racist who blamed the Jews for Germany's problems.

Pass Document officially known as a reference book which until 1986 had to be carried by all Africans over the age of 16. It indicated whether the bearer was legally allowed in a "white" area. Africans from "independent" Bantustans carry Bantustan passports.

Second World War It lasted from 1939-45. Germany, Italy and Japan fought against Britain, the United States, the Soviet Union, France, Australia, New Zealand and others. South Africa fought as part of the British Empire.

Vigilantes In the South African context, right-wing thugs (mainly black) who act as apartheid's private army in attacking anti-apartheid activists.

White Apartheid term for all those not classified black. Previous term was European. The "whites" are regarded as one national group despite major language and cultural differences, while the blacks are divided not only into Africans, Asians (or Indians) and coloureds, but the Africans are subdivided into ten separate "nations". The term white is defined in many laws.

Index

Photographic Credits:
Pages 2-3, 22-23, 24-25, 33 left and back cover: Topham Picture Source; pages 4-5 top and 11: Mary Evans Picture Library; page 4-5 bottom: Eve Arnold, Magnum Photos; pages 6-7, 26 top and bottom and 29: Frank Spooner Pictures; pages 8-9, 9, 10-11, 12, 14-15, 14 left and right, 16, 16-17, 17, 18-19, 19, 20-21, 22-23, 31, 32 bottom and 33 centre: International Defence & Aid Fund for Southern Africa; pages 13 and 33 right: The Hutchison Library; pages 24 and 32 top: Popperfoto; front cover and pages 27 and 28: Rex Features; page 28-29: Planet Earth Pictures.

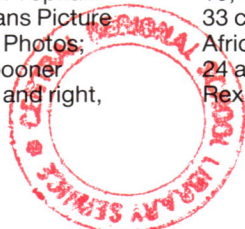

PRINTED IN BELGIUM BY
proost
INTERNATIONAL BOOK PRODUCTION